NOT

grafted in

by

Terence D. McLean

Scripture quotations in this book are from the King James Bible, God's perfectly preserved words.
(Modern spelling of the words "graff" and "graffed" as found in the King James Bible are "graft" and "grafted" but the meanings are exactly the same and this book uses them interchangeably.)

Discerning The Times Publishing Co., Inc.
Post Office Box 87
Alpha OH 45301-0087

International Standard Book Number
ISBN-13: 978-0-978963-7-7
ISBN-10: 0-9789863-7-7

ISBN-13: 978-0-9789863-7-7
ISBN-10: 0-9789863-7-7
9 0 0 0 0
9 780978 986377

Grafting is done for a reason.

Thomas Jefferson wrote in 1818:

"we know that the grafting art implants a new tree on the savage stock..."

...which means the purpose of grafting is to create a better plant that produces superior fruit.

The trunk of the tree (called the stock) may be sturdy (savage) and long-lived, but if it does not produce fruit, the tree is of little value. By grafting productive branches (called scion) into the stock, the result is a sturdy tree that bears fruit.

For obvious reasons, no horticulturist would graft an unpredictable wild branch into a sturdy stock; but that is exactly what God does:

"...thou, being a wild olive tree, wert graffed in among them, and with them partakest of the root and fatness of the olive tree;" Romans 11:17

God takes what had been a perfectly good "stock" (Old Testament Israel) and grafts something "wild" into it: very much the opposite of proper horticultural procedure. What the Lord knows is that Israel (for the most part) rejected its Messiah, but that God's promises and covenants with Israel are everlasting; so the Lord grafts in the "wild olive branch" so as to preserve Israel's stock into "thy kingdom come."

Almost every scholar who has ever commented on Romans Chapter Eleven believes the "wild olive branches" to be Gentile Christians being grafted into Israel's "root and fatness" which gives rise to the thinking that Christianity is Jewish and that by being grafted into Israel's roots, Christians get Israel's spiritual or physical blessings, or both their physical and spiritual blessings.

Since the Bible describes Christians as a "new creature," grafting them into old Israel is problematic. Christians are a "new man" and "one body" in which "there is neither Jew nor Greek," hardly terms befitting the church as a spiritual or replacement Israel.

3

Shelves filled with books written by scores of notable scholars present today's Christian churches as the "wild olive branches;" but this one unpretentious little book corrects their errors, advances dispensational understanding, and gives the proper reading and exposition of the passages involved: see if you agree.

Olive trees, fig trees and vines are three different plants representing three different things.

The vine identifies the national house of Israel:

"For the vineyard of the LORD of hosts is the house of Israel, and the men of Judah his pleasant plant:" Isaiah 5:7 (What doctrine might you expect in a church calling itself "The Vineyard?")

The fig shows up in the Garden in Eden as Adam's unacceptable covering, which God replaces with an animal's skin. The fig represents man's attempts at self-righteous religion, a lesson that Able learned but a lesson which escaped Cain.

The Messiah to Israel said "... Behold, these three years I come seeking fruit on this fig tree, and find none: cut it down; why cumbereth it the ground?" Luke 13:7 For three years Christ had ministered to the lost sheep of the House of Israel (the vine) looking for fruit (figs) and found none. (This of course must mean that Matthew 24 is not about Israel becoming a nation in 1948).

The olive is associated with olive oil which was used in lamps producing light:

"Command the children of Israel, that they bring unto thee pure oil olive beaten for the light, to cause the lamps to burn continually." Leviticus 24:2

Although it is commonly taught that olive oil

4

is a type of the anointing by the Holy Spirit of God, the Bible indicates otherwise:

"Thou shalt have olive trees throughout all thy coasts, but thou shalt not anoint thyself with the oil; for thine olive shall cast his fruit." Deuteronomy 28:40

Olive oil was used to produce light and Christ identified Himself as being the light that olive oil typified:

"Then spake Jesus again unto them, saying, I am the light of the world: he that followeth me shall not walk in darkness, but shall have the light of life." John 8:12

To reject the Messiah was to walk in darkness, but there were a few who accepted the Messiah and walked in the light: "But if we walk in the light, as he is in the light, we have fellowship one with another, and the blood of Jesus Christ his Son cleanseth us from all sin." 1 John 1:7

The Sadducees and Pharisees walked in darkness as did the priests and the scribes. They rejected their Messiah and they conspired to have Christ crucified.

But there were some walking in the light, some who testified that Christ was the prophesied Messiah by being baptized with John's baptism with water:

"And all the people that heard him, and the publicans, justified God, being baptized with the baptism of John. But the Pharisees and lawyers rejected the counsel of God against themselves, being not baptized of him." Luke 7:29-30

The purpose of John's baptism had been stated:

"This is he of whom I said, After me cometh a man which is preferred before me: for he was before me. And I knew him not: but that he should be made manifest to Israel, therefore am I come baptizing with water." John 1:30-31

What we have then is the "stock" of Old Testament Israel being found unworthy, walking in darkness:

"Yet I had planted thee a noble vine, wholly a right seed: how then art thou turned into the degenerate plant of a strange vine unto me?" Jeremiah 2:21

For thousands of years Old Testament Israel had been viable as God's chosen people, but their Messiah found them almost universally in unbelief; yet God's promises to Israel must be fulfilled.

It is at this point that God breaks off the unbelieving branches (unbelieving Israel) and replaces them by grafting in the remnant of (believing) Israel that had received Christ as Messiah.

God's promises to Israel were never to the Gentiles (unless Gentiles proselytized into Israel), and so it would have been wrong to graft Gentiles into Israel's stock:

"That at that time ye were without Christ, being aliens from the commonwealth of Israel, and strangers from the covenants of promise, having no hope, and without God in the world:" Ephesians 2:12

At this point, perhaps the most wise thing would be to ask "...For what saith the scripture?" Romans 4:3

And that is exactly what we are about to study:

Israel is Paul's focus...

in Romans chapters nine, ten and eleven. They were never far from his mind in the fist eight chapters and he even spoke directly to them at times: ("Behold, thou art called a Jew, and restest in the law, and makest thy boast of God," Romans 2:17). Paul's focus, however, was not entirely upon Israel until chapter nine.

Romans 9:3-4 "...my kinsmen according to the flesh: Who are Israelites; to whom pertaineth the adoption, and the glory, and the covenants, and the giving of the law, and the service of God, and the promises;"

Saul of Tarsus had rejected Israel's Messiah and had persecuted Peter's Little Flock of Israel that had received Christ. When Saul was converted by Christ Himself in Acts chapter nine, Saul became Paul and Paul became burdened for the people of Israel who remained in the unbelief Paul had once shared.

Romans 10:1 "Brethren, my heart's desire and prayer to God for Israel is, that they might be saved."

Thousands of Jews who had rejected Christ repented of their error and joined with Peter and believing Israel in the early part of the book of Acts. Most, however, continued in unbelief.

Stephen preached to unbelieving Israel in Acts chapter seven and declared the unbelieving Jew as being no better than a Gentile:

"Ye stiffnecked and uncircumcised in heart and ears, ye do always resist the Holy Ghost: as your fathers did, so do ye." Acts 7:51

It is the "uncircumcised in heart and ears" to whom Paul speaks in Romans chapters nine, ten and eleven. The Hebrew people who had accepted Christ as Messiah were not Paul's concern, but rather the unbelievers.

The Gentiles had always been "uncircumcised in heart and ears" and Paul was their apostle (Romans 11:13).

The people of Israel who had rejected their Messiah were judged to be similarly "uncircumcised in heart and ears;" and they constituted a particular concern for Paul since he had been just like them, and not that long ago.

Paul wanted to see his kinsmen according to the flesh saved.

"...For they are not all Israel, which are of Israel:" Romans 9:6

And that meant Paul's "kinsmen according to the flesh" thought they were the "Israel of God" but were actually the "broken off branches."

Paul wanted to provoke unbelieving Israel to receive Christ as their prophesied Messiah and to be part of the wild olive branch that God would graft in to the root and fatness which was Covenant Israel.

Separate from Paul's provocative message to Israel, Christ had appointed Paul to preach the gospel of the grace of God to the Gentiles.

Peter preached the gospel of the Kingdom (Matthew 10:5-6), attempted to prevent the crucifixion of Christ from taking place (Matthew 16:21-23), and preached the cross as a murder indictment (Acts 2:23). Paul preached the gospel of the grace of God which centers on expiation by the crucifixion (I Corinthians 15:1-4) and glories in the cross (Galatians 6:14).

Those people, who have yet to learn that the gospel of the Kingdom and the gospel of the grace of God are as different as are God's earthly people (Israel) and God's heavenly people (the Body of Christ), are ill-equipped to exposit the grafting-in passages because they have conflated the new creature (body of Christ) with the new covenant people (Israel)

Dispensationalists who wrongly conflate the twelve apostles with the body of Christ (e.g.: Cornelius R. Stam) are no help in that they come to the same wrong conclusion by combining everything rather than rightly dividing anything.

To bring the people who have yet to learn that the gospel of the Kingdom and the gospel of the grace of God are different up to speed would require a commentary on the entire book of Romans, which this is not.

To respond to every wrong thing that has been said or written about the grafting-in passages would require a library and a lifetime. Rather than that, let us...

Look at the verses...

If by any means I may provoke to emulation them which are my flesh, and might save some of them. Romans 11:14

Unbelieving Israel could be provoked so that some might be saved; and that is what Paul wanted to accomplish.

The very word "emulate" involves wanting to be equal with or to imitate a standard previously established. Since the Body of Christ is a new creature complete in Christ, there would be no point in its emulating anything.

Gentiles, try as they might, could not emulate that in which they had no part. (Ephesians 2:12)

The only thing that makes sense would be for Paul to provoke unbelieving Israel (the broken off branches) to emulate Peter's "little flock" of believing Israel and thereby become part of the wild olive branch which could be grafted in.

For if the casting away of them be the reconciling of the world, what shall the receiving of them be, but life from the dead? Romans 11:15

Clearly, by Israel's fall, the world could be reconciled. "I say then... through their fall salvation is come unto the Gentiles, for to provoke them to jealousy." Romans 11:11

Being grafted in to that which had fallen so that salvation could come to the ones grafted in to the fallen, to provoke the fallen to jealousy of the ones who had been grafted in is not simply circular reasoning, it is utter nonsense.

In the four gospels and the book of Acts, there are two Israels: believing and unbelieving. Israel's believers had received Christ as Messiah and became part of Peter's "little flock" as in: "Fear not, little flock; for it is your Father's good pleasure to give you the kingdom." Luke 12:32

They were all set.

Israel's unbelievers were broken off branches that would be cast into the fire: "but he will burn up the chaff with unquenchable fire." Matthew 3:12

Unbelieving Israel needed to be provoked to jealousy so as to receive Christ as Messiah and join with Peter's "little flock" of Hebrew believers, for they would be grafted in to the root and fatness of Covenant Israel.

The Gentiles had no part in either the stock of the olive tree or the scion that would be grafted in. The Gentiles are not a scion that will march in to Zion. They are a new creature headed for heavenly places.

For if the firstfruit be holy, the lump is also holy: and if the root be holy, so are the branches. And if some of the branches be broken off, and thou, being a wild olive tree, wert graffed in among them, and with them partakest of the root and fatness of the olive tree; Romans 11:16-17

We are not the wild olives branches grafted in to the root and fatness of Israel. Rather, the wild olive branches are those who received Christ as Messiah.

Before the cross, before the revelation of the Pauline mystery, before the gospel of the grace of God instituted a new creature headed for heavenly places, the Lord Jesus Christ said to Israel: "Therefore say I unto you, The kingdom of God

shall be taken from you, and given to a na[t]
bringing forth the fruits thereof." Matthew 21:4[3]

As shocking as this idea may be to the c[o]
temporary reader, what you are considering here
hardly new or ground-breaking. In 1926, Georg[e]
Williams wrote in his Student's Commentary o[n]
the Holy Scriptures, page 870, "That wild olive tre[e]
is not the church."

We should not find it strange that truth tra-
vails as it travels through time: "And judgment is
turned away backward, and justice standeth afar
off: for truth is fallen in the street, and equity cannot enter." Isaiah 59:14

Way back in 1917, The Scofield Reference Bible, page 1252, boldly stated "In his (Paul's) writ-
ings alone we find the doctrine, position, walk, and
destiny of the church." The simple truth of that
statement continues to be a "truth fallen in the
street" nearly a century later.

Perhaps the greatest hindrance to advancing
Bible truth is that there are so few Bible students;
but what of the teachers and pastors, what of the
seminaries and denominations?

Perhaps the common denominator would be
our selfishness: we fail to distinguish between Israel and the Body of Christ because we want every
promise of God for ourselves. Interestingly, however, we are content to leave the curses (as in Deuteronomy 28) to Israel.

We want the heavenly places and the earthly
kingdom: we want it all, and that prejudices our
reading of passages such as these.

Boast not against the branches. But if thou
boast, thou bearest not the root, but the root thee.
Thou wilt say then, The branches were broken off,
that I might be graffed in. Romans 11:18-19

Christ came to the lost sheep of the house of
Israel; and although they rejected Him, they were

...at nation "not reckoned among the na-
...mbers 23:9) Even as lost sheep, they
...sented those chosen people with whom
made everlasting covenants.
...nce the lost sheep had not kept their part of
...ovenants, Christ has the kingdoms of this
, offered to Him by Satan. (Matthew 4:1-11,
, 4:1-13)

By Calvary's cross, God is able to leave the
.evil in the dust, right where He had placed him in
Genesis 3:14.

Christ on the cross is suspended between
heaven and earth; and by the cross Christ reclaims
the Earth as His kingdom for Israel, and by the
cross Christ institutes a new creature to reign in
heavenly places.

The root that bore the broken off branches,
the root into which wild olive branches were
grafted, that root is Israel, God's earthly people.
The Body of Christ is God's heavenly people: it
really is that simple.

"As is the earthy, such are they also that are
earthy: and as is the heavenly, such are they also
that are heavenly." 1 Corinthians 15:48

Christ's earthly kingdom is all about Israel:
"And Jesus said unto them, Verily I say unto
you, That ye which have followed me, in the regen-
eration when the Son of man shall sit in the throne
of his glory, ye also shall sit upon twelve thrones,
judging the twelve tribes of Israel." Matthew 19:28

That we won't be here during Israel's millen-
nial kingdom should be obvious:
Ephesians 1:3 "Blessed be the God and Father of our Lord Jesus Christ, who hath blessed us
with all spiritual blessings in heavenly places in
Christ:"

Rather than bringing in the kingdom, we are
to "Set your affection on things above, not on
things on the earth." Colossians 3:2

"There are also celestial bodies, and terrestrial: but the glory of the celestial is on the glory of the terrestrial is another." 1 thians 15:40

Our celestial bodies would be wasted earth.

"There is neither Jew nor Greek... for ye all one in Christ Jesus" (Galatians 3:28) does accommodate twelve thrones and twelve tri and when you see these simple truths, you won how it is you ever missed them.

Here's how it happened:

We were not taught that every verse of th Bible has three applications: historical, spiritua and doctrinal.

Every verse is historically true, and so anyon at any time can approach the Bible knowing it is a historically accurate.

Every verse has a spiritualized application, and so we can learn that obedience to God is important without (for example) actually building an ark.

Building the ark, getting on board with the animals and disembarking after the flood would be the literal hands-on doctrinal application of those verses.

We were not taught to distinguish between the spiritual and the doctrinal application of Bible verses, and that resulted in our failing to note doctrinal distinctions. How else might we explain reciting the so-called "Lord's Prayer" when it is about Israel's earthly kingdom coming down while we are headed up, for heavenly places?

How else might we explain reading the twenty-third Psalm at a funeral when that chapter is all about Israel's surviving the Great Tribulation and entering into its kingdom?

How else might we explain teaching the tithe when we are not under the law but under grace?

ıse of unbelief they were broken ındest by faith. Be not highminded, ;od spared not the natural branches, . he also spare not thee. Romans

,d been talking to and about Israel ever ıs chapter nine; and here it is clear that king to the people for whom the fear of the beginning of wisdom because we ı: "God hath not given us the spirit of Timothy 1:7)

ɔelieving Israel stood in stark contrast to ɟ Israel in all four gospels and early Acts, ıas unbelieving Israel that is represented by ıken off branches. They were the natural ıes, but God did not spare them, because of ınbelief.

The disciples and their converts, both Jew Gentile, were to be grafted in; and with that God could keep His promises to the good olive , Old Testament Israel, even though the natural nches were broken off.

Generally speaking, those who believe it is ıe Gentile church, the Body of Christ, which is ɟrafted in to Israel's good olive tree rest that belief upon Romans 11:17-18, which we have already discussed.

Bible commentaries, teachers and expositors who rightly note that Romans chapters nine, ten and eleven are all about Paul's evaluation of Israel's condition invariably vacate that truth so as to invest today's church with Israel's promises by wresting those two verses from their context. We'll not be doing that.

Not surprisingly, many of those teachers and writers do the exact some thing with: "That if thou shalt confess with thy mouth the Lord Jesus, and shalt believe in thine heart that God hath raised him from the dead, thou shalt be saved. For with the heart man believeth unto righteousness; and with the mouth confession is made unto salvation." Romans 10:9-10

Saying words, confessing with the mouth, is a work. We are saved by grace through faith and not by works. Saying words is a work, yet people who ought to know better present Romans 10:9-10 as part of the plan of salvation, which it is not.

Romans 10:1 is to and about Israel, as are verses 2, 3, 4, 5, 6, 7, and 8. Suddenly, however, you are to think verses 9 and 10 are yours; but then it's right back to Israel for the remainder of chapter ten. Wresting verses from their context is hardly the way to preach or teach, much less evangelize.

Israel would have understood the importance of such confession:

Matthew 10:32 "Whosoever therefore shall confess me before men, him will I confess also before my Father which is in heaven."

Luke 12:8 "Also I say unto you, Whosoever shall confess me before men, him shall the Son of man also confess before the angels of God:"

We should know better:

Ephesians 2:8-9 "For by grace are ye saved through faith; and that not of yourselves: it is the gift of God: Not of works, lest any man should boast."

Romans 5:1 "Therefore being justified by faith, we have peace with God through our Lord Jesus Christ:"

Two true stories illustrate this point:

One dear lady responded to the "invitation" at the end of a service because she wanted to be saved. The preacher told her to pray that God would forgive her sins because she had trusted Christ's payment for her sins.

After the lady had prayed, the preacher said

to her, "Did you ask the Lord to forgive your sins?" to which she replied "Yes, sir."

"Well," the preacher asked, "What did the Lord say?"

"He said 'Oakee doakee," was her answer.

If confessing with one's mouth is required, does "Oakee doakee" validate what was confessed? And what if you confess with the wrong words?

A handsome young man in his mid-twenties responded to the "invitation" and afterward the preacher asked Him if Christ had forgiven his sins.

"Damn right."

If that young man had trusted Christ's death-burial-resurrection as payment for his sins, did he make the cross of Christ of none effect by cursing when he confessed with his mouth?

Either it is grace through faith in what Christ accomplished or it is our works: make up your mind. And if you must confess with your mouth, do "Oakee doakee" and "Damn right" qualify?

Saying words, confessing with your mouth, is a work of the flesh, not of grace, nor of faith.

Romans 11:6 "And if by grace, then is it no more of works: otherwise grace is no more grace. But if it be of works, then is it no more grace: otherwise work is no more work."

This all serves as an excellent example of failing to distinguish between the spiritual application of a verse and the doctrinal application of that same verse. Romans 10:9-10 became a part of something called "The Romans Road" presentation of the gospel; but by adding a works requirement of saying words, it wasn't a presentation of the gospel of the grace of God at all.

Romans chapter ten is about Israel's confessing Christ as Messiah, which they had refused to do in the gospels. It is not about today's unsaved sinners saying words.

Note the difference:

"In whom ye also trusted, after that ye heard the word of truth, the gospel of your salvation: in whom also after that ye believed, ye were sealed with that holy Spirit of promise," Ephesians 1:13

We hear the gospel of our salvation, how that Christ died for our sins, we trust the gospel that we heard from the word of truth (I Corinthians 15:1-4), and our salvation is sealed.

But now, back to the grafting in issue:

Behold therefore the goodness and severity of God: on them which fell, severity; but toward thee, goodness, if thou continue in his goodness: otherwise thou also shalt be cut off. Romans 11:22

To all of you who believe yourselves to be eternally secure: out of the pool, for whoever you think the grafted in branches are, it is clear from this verse that their standing is conditional and not complete in Christ.

Those who believe they cannot lose their salvation are either ignorant of this verse or intellectually dishonest about being grafted in, because there can be no doubt that this verse will only work for Armenians, covenantalists, Pentecostals, and others who have failed to rightly divide the word of truth.

The Lord Jesus Christ, according to the gospel of the grace of God, bore the severity of God in my place. II Corinthians 5:21 "For he hath made him to be sin for us, who knew no sin; that we might be made the righteousness of God in him."

As a result of Christ's propitiatory sacrifice, God is no longer imputing trespasses upon us (II Corinthians 5:19 '"To wit, that God was in Christ, reconciling the world unto himself, not imputing their trespasses unto them; and hath committed unto us the word of reconciliation") because God already imputed all trespasses upon Christ.

To have good standing as a grafted in branch be conditional upon an "if" is not a new concept to Israel because their covenant relationship with God is very much an "if...then" situation.

For example:

"Now therefore, **if** ye will obey my voice indeed, and keep my covenant, **then** ye shall be a peculiar treasure unto me above all people: for all the earth is mine:" Exodus 19:5

"**If** my people, which are called by my name, shall humble themselves, and pray, and seek my face, and turn from their wicked ways; **then** will I hear from heaven, and will forgive their sin, and will heal their land." II Chronicles 7:14

Salvation by grace through faith is not "iffy" because it is God's doing without our needing to perform. We are complete in Christ (Colossians 2:9 -10), God is no longer angry at us (Romans 5:1) because we are accepted in the beloved (Ephesians 1:6) in that we are crucified with Christ (Galatians 2:20) and are henceforth a new creature (II Corinthians 5:17). God's grace is sufficient, whether you think so or not.

You might debate what "If thou continue in his goodness" (Romans 11:22) would entail: baptism, commandment keeping, the golden rule, enduring to the end or whatever else; yet there can be no debate that the verse teaches the grafted in branches can be cut off just as unbelieving Israel had been cut off.

If you believe in the security of the believer, complete in Christ, it is not possible to also believe you are a grafted in branch: they are mutually exclusive because the grafted in branch is neither complete nor secure.

If you believe you can lose your salvation It makes sense that you would believe you are among the grafted in branches because your entire belief system is centered on Israel's promises: you probably are unsaved.

The Body of Christ in this, the dispensation of God's grace, cannot be cut off, cannot be separated from the love of Christ.   (Romans 8:35, 38, 39, Ephesians 1:13-14, 4:30).

And they also, if they abide not still in unbelief, shall be graffed in: for God is able to graff them in again. For if thou wert cut out of the olive tree which is wild by nature, and wert graffed contrary to nature into a good olive tree: how much more shall these, which be the natural branches, be graffed into their own olive tree? Romans 11:23-24

After making is clear that the broken off branches could be grafted in again contingent upon their faith, Paul then advances an hypothetical example involving the wild olive tree, not the new creature, not the Body of Christ.

Pastor Cornelius R. Stam gets this part right in his commentary on Romans, page 279 when he says: "Could the grafted-in branches, then, represent the Church, the Body of Christ, as some teach? Again, no." Unfortunately, Stam did not quit when he was ahead because Stam then took the twelve apostles and placed them in the Body of Christ, leaving Stam with no wild olive branches to graft.

C. I. Scofield died in 1917, Clarence Larkin in 1924, and it is fair to say the fundamentalist Baptists have not advanced much since then.

As time goes by, it is likely we will discern that since the death of C. F. Baker in 1994 and C. R. Stam in 2003, mid-Acts dispensationalism has lacked leadership and lost ground as well.

Understanding these passages is very simple: Peter, his little flock of Hebrew believers, and gentile converts such as Cornelius (Acts 10) would be partaking of the root and fatness of the good olive tree, even if the Gentiles were not circumcised,

19

even though the Little Flock of Israel had followed the Messiah rather than the Scribes and Pharisees.

Careful readers of the text will also note that both the broken-off branches grafted in again and the wild olive branches grafted in are both "grafted in to their own olive tree..." No new creature there, no Body of Christ, no "old things are passed away." (II Corinthians 5:17)

As we come to Romans 11:25-28 we are well past the proof-texter's territory: all they really wanted was verse 17 so as to advance their agenda.

Proof-texting involves selecting an agenda and then looking for verses to advance that agenda.

To illustrate, let us suppose our agenda is to tell our audience that God is going to take care of their needs. We might start with:

"Surely goodness and mercy shall follow me all the days of my life: and I will dwell in the house of the LORD for ever." Psalm 23:6

Disregarding:

"For I reckon that the sufferings of this present time are not worthy to be compared with the glory which shall be revealed in us." Romans 8:18

Then we might advance our agenda with:

"Give us this day our daily bread." Matthew 6:11

Disregarding:

"For even when we were with you, this we commanded you, that if any would not work, neither should he eat." II Thessalonians 3:10

Then we might wrap it up with:

"I have been young, and now am old; yet have I not seen the righteous forsaken, nor his seed begging bread." Psalm 37:25

Disregarding:

"In journeyings often, in perils of waters, in perils of robbers, in perils by mine own countrymen, in perils by the heathen, in perils in the city, in perils in the wilderness, in perils in the sea, in perils among false brethren;" II Corinthians 11:26

Rather than allowing the agenda to determine the verse selection, allegorizing, spiritualizing and telling stories as we go, we must learn which verses apply to us doctrinally and then traffic among them.

We noted back on page thirteen that every verse of the Bible has three applications, but that was not enough. We must also be able to determine to whom the doctrine in each individual verse applies. There is a three-point test that helps with that:

1. Who is speaking?
2. To whom?
3. Are we in the audience to whom the verse is directed?

To illustrate:

"If my people, which are called by my name, shall humble themselves, and pray, and seek my face, and turn from their wicked ways; then will I hear from heaven, and will forgive their sin, and will heal their land." II Chronicles 7:14

Ezra the Scribe wrote both books which chronicle the historical events and narratives involving Jehovah God's first-born son, Israel.

The audience for II Chronicles 7:14 was the Hebrew people, who could read the material and learn their history from Adam through the destruction of Jerusalem by Nebuchadnezzar.

Completed at least four centuries before Christ, oriented entirely toward Israel under the law, II Chronicles 7:14 cannot possibly have any doctrine for us in the Body of Christ in this dispensation of God's grace.

On an historical level, what the books of Chronicles records no doubt took place.

On a spiritual level we can see God's care and provision for His people, although in this verse we would not have been His people. (Ephesians 2:12)

On a doctrinal level, the people to whom this verse applies get their sins forgiven without the blood of Christ, which cannot be us. (Ephesians 1:7, 2:13, Colossians 1:14)

Preachers have used II Chronicles 7:14 for decades in their attempt to advance their agenda of getting the land (America) healed. The plain fact that things continue to get worse and worse as the years pass should have been a clue to someone that there was a problem, not with the verse of course, but with its misapplication.

Now we come to the verses that make it crystal clear that the grafted in cannot be the Body of Christ. Since the proof-texter was only interested in verse 17 so as to advance his agenda and maintain his prejudices and predilections, these verses escaped his attention.

For I would not, brethren, that ye should be ignorant of this mystery, lest ye should be wise in your own conceits; that blindness in part is happened to Israel, until the fulness of the Gentiles be come in.   Romans 11:25

How is it the Gentiles who think they have been grafted in would deny that they are blind? Since this verse declares Israel is blind and since Romans 11:11 declared Israel fallen, why would being grafted in be considered a good thing?

"...through their fall salvation is come unto the Gentiles, for to provoke them to jealousy." (Romans 11:11) makes it clear that for saved people to have been grafted in as if they were fallen and blind Israel makes no sense at all.

Understanding what Paul means when he says "that blindness in part has happened to Israel" is very simple indeed: "in part" means not the

22

whole. Some did receive Christ as Messiah and they were the ones grafted in to the root and fatness of God's covenants and promises to His chosen people.

We know that in Christ "there is neither Jew nor Greek" (Galatians 3:28, Colossians 3:11), and we know "Jews require a sign" and we know Greeks seek after wisdom (I Corinthians 1:22); but we now know that we are neither Jew nor Greek when we are saved and in Christ: we are a new creature, complete in Christ, not grafted in.

Paul refers to this truth as a "mystery" about which we should not be ignorant, but ignorance of the Pauline mysteries remains pervasive:

Paul's mysteries revealed

1. Romans 11:11-25: Israel is fallen, blind, and has no standing.
2. I Corinthians 12:13, II Corinthians 5:17: a new creature, neither Jew nor Gentile has been created.
3. Colossians 1:25-28, Ephesians 3:1-10: The Body of Christ has standing and is God's agency as ambassadors with the word of reconciliation.
4. Ephesians 1:9-10, Colossians 1:16: God's purpose for all his creation is revealed.
5. Romans 3:24-25, 6:14, Ephesians 2:8-9: Christ paid for all sin with His death, burial and resurrection without the works of the law.
6. I Corinthians 15:51-56, I Thessalonians 4:13-18: the Body of Christ will reside in heavenly places and will not reign with Christ and Israel on the Earth.

Paul uses the word "ignorant" ten times, and all but one of them relate to Paul's revelation of the mystery. Typically, the same people who are ignorant of Paul's mysteries claim to be the grafted wild olive branches, recipients of Israel's covenants and promises. (Ephesians 2:12)

And so all Israel shall be saved: as it is written, There shall come out of Sion the Deliverer, and shall turn away ungodliness from Jacob: Romans 11:26

As Paul concludes his three chapter lesson dealing with Israel, he quotes Joel 3:16 and Psalm 14:7, making the statement that "all Israel shall be saved."

It could not be that the grafted in branches were anything other than Israel; and it certainly would be wrong to think that the Body of Christ, in which there is neither Jew nor Greek would be included with or as Jacob.

The body of Christ, complete in Christ, recipient of Christ's imputed righteousness, would not be needing to turn away ungodliness.

But it gets even easier:

For this is my covenant unto them, when I shall take away their sins. Romans 11:27

"Them" would not be "us," but it would be Israel.

We who are saved members of the Body of Christ already have had our sins dealt with and need not wait until some future time.

Romans 5:9 "Much more then, being now justified by his blood, we shall be saved from wrath through him."

When unbelieving Jews repented and were baptized by Peter in Acts Chapter Two, he tells them about their future expiation of sin:

Acts 3:19 "Repent ye therefore, and be converted, that your sins may be blotted out, when the times of refreshing shall come from the presence of the Lord;"

1 Peter 1:13 "Wherefore gird up the loins of

24

your mind, be sober, and hope to the end for the grace that is to be brought unto you at the revelation of Jesus Christ;"

God had made His covenant with Israel, and the promise of forgiveness of their sins was part of His promise to them:

Jeremiah 31:34 ..."for I will forgive their iniquity, and I will remember their sin no more."

In the context of:

Jeremiah 31:31 "Behold, the days come, saith the LORD, that I will make a new covenant with the house of Israel, and with the house of Judah:" which most Christians wrongly believe to be their church. They will call themselves "New Testament Christians" when there is no such thing in their Bible, and many will go so far as to claim to have Israel's anointing.

We are not the "house of Israel... house of Judah" of the Old Testament and neither are we the "house of Israel... house of Judah" of the New Testament (Hebrews 8:8-10). We are the church of what's happening now.

But let us engage in considering that this little booklet might be mistaken, that the grafted in branches are today's Gentile church, grafted in to Israel's root and fatness.

Romans 11:17 And if some of the branches be broken off, and thou, being a wild olive tree, wert graffed in among them, and with them partakest of the root and fatness of the olive tree;

Of Romans 11:17, John Calvin said "he now refers to the present dignity of the Gentiles"

Adam Clark said "The word *thou* here is used to denote the *Gentile*"

John Wesley said "Thou– O gentile, being a wild olive tree..."

Matthew Poole said "by *the olive tree* he means the church of Christ..."

William Newell said "...we as Gentiles, have been set in the place of blessing from Abraham..."

John Gill said "...the gospel church is so

called because of its excellency..."

Matthew Poole said "by the olive tree he means the church of Christ... by the fatness of the olive tree he means all the promises and privileges, the graces and ordinances, the spiritual blessings and benefits,"

Clearly those who would disagree with this booklet are many and renowned. More recent writers also disagree:

Peter S. Ruckman said "The wild olive tree is the Gentiles. They are put onto the good olive tree by faith in Jesus Christ."

J. Vernon McGee said "You and I benefit because of the nation Israel."

Finis Jennings Dake said "Some are broken off because of their unbelief and Gentiles take their place to partake of Israel's blessings."

We could fill a dozen pages listing all those who believe the grafted in entity to be today's church; but what of Romans 11:28? If the grafted in is today's church, why would they be declared to be an enemy of the gospel?

As concerning the gospel, they are enemies for your sakes: but as touching the election, they are beloved for the fathers' sakes. Romans 11:28

Israel: root, stock, branches, broken off branches, grafted in branches... all of Israel are enemies of Paul's gospel of God's grace in this, the dispensation of God's grace. And it must follow that all the people who think they are Israel are enemies of salvation by Paul's gospel, preferring good works, baptism and law-keeping.

Israel: root, stock, branches, broken off branches, grafted in branches... all of Israel are the elect of God, beloved for the father's sake.

Isaiah 45:4 "For Jacob my servant's sake, and <u>Israel mine elect</u>, I have even called thee by thy name: I have surnamed thee, though thou hast not known me."

But almost no one knows that there is more than one gospel in the Bible. And almost no one knows that only Israel and Christ are "the elect." And that explains why almost no one agrees that the Body of Christ has no part in the root, stock or branches which are all about Israel.

The fact is Peter, James and John were preaching the gospel of the kingdom knowing nothing of the benefits of Christ's cross:
"For he taught his disciples, and said unto them, The Son of man is delivered into the hands of men, and they shall kill him; and after that he is killed, he shall rise the third day. But they under-stood not that saying, and were afraid to ask him." Mark 9:31-32
"Let these sayings sink down into your ears: for the Son of man shall be delivered into the hands of men. But they understood not this saying, and it was hid from them, that they perceived it not: and they feared to ask him of that saying." Luke 9:44-45
"For he shall be delivered unto the Gentiles, and shall be mocked, and spitefully entreated, and spitted on: And they shall scourge him, and put him to death: and the third day he shall rise again. And they understood none of these things: and this saying was hid from them, neither knew they the things which were spoken." Luke 18:32-34

Rather than "looking forward to the cross," Peter actually wanted to prevent the crucifixion from taking place:
"From that time forth began Jesus to shew unto his disciples, how that he must go unto Jeru-salem, and suffer many things of the elders and chief priests and scribes, and be killed, and be raised again the third day. Then Peter took him, and began to rebuke him, saying, Be it far from

thee, Lord: this shall not be unto thee." Matthew 16:21-22

Rather than glorying in the cross (Galatians 6:14) and preaching the cross (I Corinthians 2:2), Christ's disciples were preaching the gospel of the kingdom, knowing nothing of the benefits of the cross.

"For as yet they knew not the scripture, that he must rise again from the dead." John 20:9

Making matters even worse, most people who read Romans think of themselves as being the "elect" when only Israel and Christ qualify for that title.

Christ: "Behold my servant, whom I uphold; mine elect, in whom my soul delighteth; I have put my spirit upon him: he shall bring forth judgment to the Gentiles." Isaiah 42:1

Israel: For Jacob my servant's sake, and Israel mine elect, I have even called thee by thy name: I have surnamed thee, though thou hast not known me. Isaiah 45:4

When today's Christian mixes the Cross of Christ with the kingdom gospel, it is inevitable that he will think himself to be at one with Israel.

When today's Christian identifies himself as the "elect," he invariable thinks he is Israel.

When today's Christian believes himself to be grafted in to Israel's olive tree, becoming recipient of Israel's root and fatness, he must of necessity believe himself to be Israel.

What that means, of course, is that today's Christian is "Christian" in name only.

Just as it is impossible to mix law with grace or to mix works with grace, it is impossible to mix the Body of Christ with Israel. We are separate: Israel will enjoy its earthly kingdom while the Body of Christ will inhabit heavenly places.

We are NOT grafted in.

The King James Bible contains God's perfectly preserved words, and over ninety-four percent of those words are about God's prophetic program for dominion on the earth.

"And in the days of these kings shall the God of heaven set up a kingdom, which shall never be destroyed: and the kingdom shall not be left to other people, but it shall break in pieces and consume all these kingdoms, and it shall stand for ever." Daniel 2:44

Less than six percent of the Bible, the thirteen books written by Paul, explain the revelation of the mystery, which includes a new creature, the Body of Christ, with dominion in heavenly places.

More than ninety-four percent of the Bible is about Israel's earthly kingdom; and way more than ninety-four percent of "Christians" have missed Paul's mystery truth and have grafted themselves into Israel's prophetic program of earthly dominion.

We are to set our affection on things above, Colossians 3:2; yet people who think they are grafted in are all about a kingdom on this earth.

We will have a body celestial, I Corinthians 15:40; yet the people who think they are grafted in are all about ruling with Christ on the earth.

We are to preach Christ and Him crucified:
"I declare unto you the gospel
...By which also ye are saved,
...how that Christ died for our sins according to the scriptures; And that he was buried, and that he rose again the third day according to the scriptures: 1 Corinthians 15:1-4

Not "repent and be baptized." Acts 2:38
Not "receive Jesus." John 1:12
Not "endure to the end." Matthew 24:13
Not "live it." John 5:28-29
Not "do unto others." Matthew 25:45-46

Trust Christ's payment for your sin.
We are NOT grafted in.

Books by Terence D. McLean:

Basics of Mid-Acts Dispensationalism
For every new believer, for everyone new to the concept of Pauline dispensationalism.
114 pages $5.00

Jesus Wasn't Talking To You
Showing the red letters belong to kingdom Israel and that Christ speaks to us through Paul.
32 pages $3.00

M. A.D. about Hebrews
Answering all the difficult questions posed in the book of Hebrews with ease and accuracy.
212 pages $8.00

Shot At And Missed
Point-blank attack on mid-Acts dispensationalism answered with no problems at all.
90 pages $5.00

History of Your Bible
Proving the King James Bible to be God's perfectly preserved words in our English language.
96 pages $5.00

With A Bible In My Hand
Award winning newspaper editorials.
138 pages $6.00

C. I. Scofield Colportage Sermons
Nine of Dr. Scofield's best sermons, annotated.
94 pages $5.00

Books by Carol M. McLean

PATTY'S MOST IMPORTANT QUESTION

It is a coloring book,
it is a great story,
it is an evangelistic tool
presenting salvation by grace
through faith so that children
will grasp the concept and be
saved at a young age.
32 pages $3.00

WHY BE GOOD?

If I'm saved and Jesus is going to take me to heaven, why
be good? If my sins are all
forgiven, why be good? This
coloring book answers the
hard questions kids ask.
32 pages $3.00

ORDER FROM:
Discerning the Times Publishing Co. Inc.
Post Office Box 87
Alpha OH 45301-0087   We will pay postage.

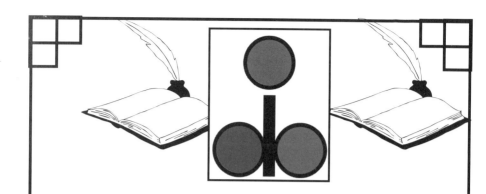

dbi
dispensational bible institute
FREE
on the internet:
www.discerningthetimespublishing.com

These video classes are recorded
in Windows Media Video (WMV) format
and are intended for high speed
Broadband (DSL, Cable, Satellite)
for play on Windows Media Player.

Dispensational Bible Institute is available
in two other formats:

1. Twenty-nine two hour DVD's to play on your
television set, DVD players and computers
for $200.00

2. An eight gigabyte flash drive for $20.00

Send your Check or Money Order to:

discerning the times
publishing co. inc.
Post Office Box 87
Alpha OH 45301